BRUNO MARS

Risa Brown

Mitchell Lane

PUBLISHERS

P.O. Box 196
Hockessin, Delaware 19707
Visit us on the web: www.mitchelllane.com

Copyright © 2016 by Mitchell Lane Publishers, Inc. All rights reserved. No part of this book may be reproduced without written permission from the publisher. Printed and bound in the United States of America.

Printing   1   2   3   4   5   6   7   8   9

A Robbie Reader Biography

Abigail Breslin
Adam Levine
Adrian Peterson
Albert Einstein
Albert Pujols
Aly and AJ
Andrew Luck
AnnaSophia Robb
Ariana Grande
Ashley Tisdale
Brenda Song
Brittany Murphy
Bruno Mars
Buster Posey
Charles Schulz
Chris Johnson
Cliff Lee
Dale Earnhardt Jr.
Darius Rucker
David Archuleta
Demi Lovato

Derrick Rose
Donovan McNabb
Drake Bell & Josh Peck
Dr. Seuss
Dwayne Johnson
Dwyane Wade
Dylan & Cole Sprouse
Emily Osment
Hilary Duff
Jamie Lynn Spears
Jennette McCurdy
Jesse McCartney
Jimmie Johnson
Joe Flacco
Jonas Brothers
Keke Palmer
Larry Fitzgerald
LeBron James
Mia Hamm
Miguel Cabrera

Miley Cyrus
Miranda Cosgrove
Philo Farnsworth
Raven-Symoné
Rixton
Robert Griffin III
Roy Halladay
Shaquille O'Neal
Story of Harley-Davidson
Sue Bird
Syd Hoff
Tiki Barber
Tim Howard
Tim Lincecum
Tom Brady
Tony Hawk
Troy Polamalu
Victor Cruz
Victoria Justice

Library of Congress Cataloging-in-Publication Data
Brown, Risa W.
Bruno Mars / by Risa Brown.
     pages cm. — (Robbie reader)
Includes bibliographical references and index.
ISBN 978-1-68020-102-4 (library bound)
1. Mars, Bruno, 1985– —Juvenile literature. 2. Musicians—United States—
Biography—Juvenile literature. I. Title.
ML3930.M318B76 2015
782.42164092—dc23
[B]
                                                                              2015003210

eBook ISBN: 978-1-68020-103-1

ABOUT THE AUTHOR: Risa Brown is the author of seventeen books for children and three for librarians. She has been a children's school librarian for twenty-three years. She wrote *Carrie Underwood*, *Blake Shelton*, and *Pitbull* for Mitchell Lane Publishers. She lives in Arlington, Texas.

PUBLISHER'S NOTE: The following story has been thoroughly researched and to the best of our knowledge represents a true story. While every possible effort has been made to ensure accuracy, the publisher will not assume liability for damages caused by inaccuracies in the data, and makes no warranty on the accuracy of the information contained herein. This story has not been authorized or endorsed by Bruno Mars.

TABLE OF CONTENTS

Words in bold type can be found in the glossary.

Bruno Mars begins the 2014 Super Bowl half-time show playing a drum set but is soon performing his signature dance moves.

Super Bowl!

At the 2014 *Super Bowl* in the middle of the field Bruno Mars appeared on the stage—as if by magic—for the **halftime show**. He sat at a green drum set. In the middle of the bass drum there was a bright red heart with the name Bernadette on it. Bruno's high energy dancing and singing made the fans dance and sing along. Everyone loved the show.

The National Football League (NFL) organizers had taken a risk with Bruno as he was the youngest star to ever perform the Super Bowl halftime show. Since he only had two albums out people wondered if he could put on a good show.

They might not have known that Bruno knew show business inside and out. He had been performing since the age of two. He had spent most of his life putting shows together. He didn't hesitate when offered the chance to do the halftime show.

What about the name Bernadette?

A few months before Bruno got the call to do the Super Bowl halftime show, his mother Bernadette died suddenly of a **brain aneurysm**. She was 55 years old and Bruno was very close to her. Bruno and his brother and sisters are a tight-knit family so Bernadette's death hit them hard, but it especially hit Bruno hard. Bernadette had been his biggest fan. She did not live long enough to see him perform in the biggest show of his life–Bruno dedicated the show to her.

He gave his all and it paid off. More people watched the halftime show than ever before. He had become a super star.

Bruno gets the crowd excited at the 2014 Super Bowl half-time show.

Bruno can do it all–sing, dance and play many musical instruments.

CHAPTER TWO

Youngest Elvis Ever

Bruno Mars' real name is Peter Gene Hernandez and he was born on October 8, 1985, in Honolulu, Hawaii. Bruno's father is also named Peter. His father organized a group called the Love Notes and his mother Bernadette was a singer. They performed in Waikiki. Bruno has four sisters: Tiara, Jamie, Presley, and Tahiti. He has one brother named Eric.

Mars' family began calling him Bruno when he was a toddler. Bruno Mars was chubby and he ran everywhere. His father thought he looked like a wrestler named Bruno Sammartino.

Early in his life, Bruno showed his love for music. He wanted to play all the musical

9

Bruno as the world's youngest Elvis Presley impersonator.

instruments at home and sing along with records, especially the songs sung by Elvis Presley. Some of the songs he heard were called doo-wop and he heard oldies but goodies from the 1950s and 1960s.

One night when Bruno was on stage during his parents' show, he did an Elvis **impersonation**. The audience loved it. Bruno loved the audience's reaction to his performance. He was hooked and he always wanted to be in the show after that. His father made a stand for Bruno so the audience could see him because Bruno was so small.

Bruno became famous for being the youngest Elvis impersonator. He was on talk shows at the age of four. At six, he was in a movie called *Honeymoon in Vegas*. In the movie, he did his regular Elvis stage show.

While he was in elementary school, Bruno and his family played to packed houses. He began learning other songs and **imitating** other artists, like pop star Michael Jackson.

But, when Bruno was 11, everything changed. He was no longer a star.

Bruno is a fashion trendsetter.

CHAPTER THREE

Hard Times

Bernadette and Peter got divorced when Bruno was just 11 years old. The band broke up and things got hard for the family.

Bruno had to change schools. Some students bullied him at his new school and called him 'Peter Pan,' among other things. Bruno did not like school because of it. He would always remember being an **outcast**. But he did not let the teasing and bullying get the best of him. He soon won everyone over.

In high school, Bruno went back to the stage. He and his band, the School Boys, continued to play oldies and he now did other impersonations. His best impersonation was of Michael Jackson. The band was the opening act for a magic show called "The Magic of Polynesia." Bruno later described it as "David Copperfield meets hula."

When Bruno graduated from Roosevelt High School, he decided to move to Los Angeles. He sent his **demo** tape to Motown Records and they wanted to meet him. They signed him to a contract, but it did not work out. Motown dropped him in less than a year.

At the time, Bruno was going by the name of Bruno Hernandez so no one knew what kind of music to expect from him. Some people thought he should change his style and be more Latino. But that was not his style. He soon adopted the name Bruno Mars.

Bruno wanted to be a singer, but he could not get any work. So he turned to songwriting to earn money. He met Philip Lawrence, who wrote lyrics and Ari Levine, who sold songs to different record companies. They called themselves the Smeezingtons. When they worked together, they would say, "This is going to be a smash," and then they would joke, "This is a smeeze." That was how they got their name.

Together the Smeezingtons wrote songs that became hits for other artists. Some were for rap artists like Cee Lo Green, Flo Rida, and B.o.B. Other songs were for pop singers like Justin Bieber. Bruno wrote "Wavin' Flag" for K'naan, which became the song for the Fédération Internationale de Football Association (FIFA) 2010 World Cup.

There were many times when Bruno was afraid he would never be a singer, but he would not give up. He kept practicing, singing, and playing.

Finally things changed.

Bruno with his songwriting team known as the Smeezingtons.

Finally Success

More and more, Bruno began doing other things besides producing hit songs for other artists. He sang with B.o.B. in "Nothin' on You" and with Travie McCoy in "Billionaire."

Those songs were on video and people began to notice Bruno's singing and his personality. He then released his solo song, "It's Better If You Don't Understand." Then he did a medley of songs at the *MTV Video Music Awards* show.

In 2010, Bruno got his album *Doo-Wops & Hooligans* ready to release in October. When the singles "Just the Way You Are" and "Grenade" were released, they were some of the best selling singles of all time. They sold well all around the world. Bruno had become an **international** hit.

Doo-wops and Hooligans was released in 2011 and sold well. Bruno recorded "It Will Rain" for the popular movie *Twilght Saga: Breaking Dawn, Part 1*. He also worked in several **collaborations** with other artists.

Hawaiians were so proud of Bruno's quick rise to fame that the governor

Bruno loves performing with his band. He is shown here with Philip Lawrence and Jamareo Artis.

announced December 19, 2011, as Bruno Mars Day. It was the last day of his sold-out three-day tour in Hawaii. After so many years of struggling, Bruno finally felt like a winner.

He began doing new things, too. He did the voice for Roberto in the movie *Rio 2*. He appeared on *Saturday Night Live* as the musical guest, and he was the host of one **episode**. He acted in the comedy sketches. He did a skit as an intern at *Pandora Radio* that showed off his ability to impersonate singers.

Bruno's next album surprised a lot of people because of its mix of styles and songs. *Unorthodox Jukebox* came out at the end of 2012 and shot to number one in many countries. Bruno soon had five number one hit singles on the *Billboard* Hot 100 at one time. The album set a record for the most number one hit singles by the same recording artist. It looked like nothing could stop Bruno Mars.

Bruno is on a roll, winning the Best Pop Vocal Album award at the Grammy Awards in 2014 for Unorthodox Jukebox.

**CHAPTER
FIVE**

Never Quit

Bruno Mars is grateful for the success he has had. All he ever wanted to do was to make music and he is doing that. For a while, he thought he might fail. Yet, he never quit.

He lives in Los Angeles with his dog, Geronimo. He bought a black older-model Cadillac with his first check; he calls the Cadillac Bessie. Since music is his life, Bruno always thinks about songs.

Bruno remains close to his family. His four sisters have formed a singing group called *Lylas*. They have a reality show with the same name. Bruno hopes to be on the *Lylas* show during the second season. His brother Eric is the drummer for Bruno's band.

Bruno shares the stage with some of the biggest names in the entertainment world.

Bruno wants to help young musicians. Working with the Grammy Foundation and the Hawaii Community Foundation, he set up a scholarship fund for music students from Hawaii. He often tells people if their dream is to make music, always work and never give up.

Every time Bruno goes to the Philippines, he visits the children at Bantay Bay. These children are victims of abuse. Bruno has also donated $100,000 to

Bruno and friends.

Bruno premieres "Uptown Funk" on Saturday Night Live.

the children who lost homes in a recent **typhoon**.

Bruno listens to stories of his fans. A loving fan in Cleveland has had a long recovery from a car accident and is still paralyzed. When Bruno heard about her struggles, he found her in the audience, hugged her, and sang "Just the Way You Are" for her.

Bruno is loved everywhere he goes. His music makes people feel good and he wants to keep doing that.

After struggling many years to make it as a singer, Bruno is now famous all over the world.

CHRONOLOGY

1985   Peter Gene Hernandez (aka Bruno Mars) was born in Honolulu, Hawaii on October 8.

1987   Peter Gene Hernandez was nicknamed Bruno.

1988   Mars joined his family's show as an Elvis impersonator.

1990   Mars appeared on *The Arsenio Hall Show*.

1992   Mars appeared in the movie *Honeymoon in Vegas*.

1997   Mars' parents divorced and his parents' band broke up.

2003   Mars graduated from Roosevelt High School. He moved to Los Angeles.

2004   Mars signed with Motown Records, but he soon lost that contract.

2005   Mars signed with Westside Independent Music Publishing to write songs. He began to work with his two friends Ari Levine and Phil Lawrence and they named their songwriting team The Smeezingtons.

2009   Mars signed with Atlanta Records as a solo artist.

2010   Mars released "Nothin' on You" and "Just the Way You Are" as singles as well as his album *Doo-Wops and Hooligans*, which reached number one on the *Billboard* Hot 100. He appeared on the *MTV Video Music Awards* show and on *Saturday Night Live* as musical guest.

2011   Mars was nominated for six Grammy awards, winning the Best Male Pop Vocal Performance award. Hawaii declared December 19 to be Bruno Mars Day.

2012   Mars released his second album *Unorthodox Jukebox*. He hosted *Saturday Night Live*.

2013   Mars released "When I Was Your Man" as a single that broke sales records. The Moonshine Jungle Tour began.

2014   Mars did the *Super Bowl XLVIII* halftime show. He won the Best Pop Vocal Album award at the *Grammy Awards*. Mars was the voice for Roberto in the movie *Rio 2*. Hawaii got another "Bruno Mars Day" ordered by Hawaii Governor Shan S. Tsutsui on April 21.

2015   The single, "UpTown Funk," became one of the best selling singles ever. Mars collaborated with Mark Ronson and the song went on to international acclaim. Mars is working on a third album.

ACCOMPLISHMENTS

Discography
2010 *Doo-Wops and Hooligans*
2012 *Unorthodox Jukebox*

Filmography
1992 *Honeymoon in Vegas*
2014 *Rio 2*

Television
2010 *Saturday Night Live* (musical guest)
2012 *The Cleveland Show* (voiceover)
2012 *Saturday Night Live* (host and musical guest)
2014 *Saturday Night Live* (musical guest)

FIND OUT MORE

Books

Higgins, Nadia. *Bruno Mars: Pop Singer and Producer.* Minneapolis, MN: Lerner, 2013.

Leavitt, Amie Jane. *Bruno Mars.* Hockessin, Del: Mitchell Lane, 2013.

Morganelli, Adriana. *Bruno Mars.* St. Catherine, ON: Crabtree, 2014.

Tieck, Sarah. *Bruno Mars: Popular Singer and Songwriter.* Minneapolis, MN: ADBO, 2012.

On the Internet

Bruno Comes Home: A Short Documentary https://www.youtube.com/watch?v=WOVfyQd_PhM

Bruno Mars aged 4: World's Youngest Elvis Impersonator. Interview. https://www.youtube.com/watch?v=tdxrOz3SZ74

"Bruno Mars." *Biography.com.* http://www.biography.com/people/bruno-mars-17162400

"Bruno Mars." *The Ellen Show.* October 2, 2014. Interview. https://www.youtube.com/watch?v=XFxm-ZEaZRs

"Celebrity Scoop: Bruno Mars." *Scholastic Action.* March 26, 2012. vol. 35, no. 12. 4-5. http://www.onlinedigitalpubs.com/publication/?i=111642&p=2

Chiu, Melody. "Bruno Mars Serenades Zumyah Thorpe." *People Magazine.* June 30, 2014. http://www.people.com/article/bruno-mars-serenades-zumyah-thorpe-concert

Guzman, Isaac. "Who Is This Bruno Mars Dude, and How Did He Get to the Super Bowl?" *Time.com.* February 3, 2014. http://time.com/5750/who-is-this-bruno-mars-dude-and-how-did-he-get-to-the-super-bowl/

Hollywood Life: Bruno Mars http://hollywoodlife.com/celeb/bruno-mars/

Joaquin, Tannya. "One-on-one with Bruno Mars' dad on his superstar son." *Hawaii New Now.* April 17, 2014. http://www.hawaiinewsnow.com/story/25279858/one-on-one-with-bruno-mars-dad-on-his-superstar-son

FIND OUT MORE

Orr, Gillian. "The Opinionated Bruno Mars." *The Independent*. December 9, 2012. http://www.independent.co.uk/arts-entertainment/music/features/meet-the-opinionated-bruno-mars-8376244.html

Works Consulted

"About Bruno Mars." *MTV*. http://www.mtv.com/artists/bruno-mars/biography/

"Bruno Mars aged 4: World's Youngest Elvis Impersonator." Interview. https://www.youtube.com/watch?v=tdxrOz3SZ74 1990 UK documentary

"Bruno Mars. *Biography.com*, http://www.biography.com/people/bruno-mars-17162400

"Bruno Mars – Coming Home Documentary." https://www.youtube.com/watch?v=WOVfyQd_PhM

Bruno Mars official website: http://www.brunomars.com/

Bruno Mars on *The Ellen Show*. October 2, 2014. Interview. https://www.youtube.com/watch?v=R9dRVCZx4ql

"Bruno Mars's 'Treasure' For Kids Affected by Typhoon Yolanda." *MYX Philippines*. March 21, 2014. http://myxph.com/features/9891/bruno-marss-treasure-for-kids-affected-by-typhoon-yolanda/

"Celebrity Scoop: Bruno Mars." *Scholastic Action*, March 26, 2012. vol. 35, no. 12, 4-5. http://www.onlinedigitalpubs.com/publication/?i=11164&p=5

Chiu, Melody. "Bruno Mars Serenades Zumyah Thorpe." *People Magazine*. June 30, 2013. http://www.people.com/article/bruno-mars-serenades-zumyah-thorpe-concert

Concepcion, Mariel. "Bruno Mars Was Once Youngest Elvis Impersonator." *Billboard*. October 29, 2010. http://www.billboard.com/articles/columns/viral-videos/952283/bruno-mars-was-once-youngest-elvis-impersonator

FIND OUT MORE

Fahy, Colette. "Bruno Mars pays loving tribute to his late mother Bernadette at Super Bowl by putting her name across a heart on his drum kit. *Daily Mail*. February 2, 2014. http://www.dailymail.co.uk/tvshowbiz/article-2550750/Bruno-Mars-pays-loving-tribute-late-mother-Bernadette-Super-Bowl-putting-heart-drum-kit.html

Fuller, Bonnie. "Bruno Mars." *Hollywood Life*. http://hollywoodlife.com/celeb/bruno-mars/

"GRAMMY Foundation Launches Bruno Mars Scholarship Fund." *GRAMMY*. February 26, 2014. http://www.grammy.com/news/grammy-foundation-launches-bruno-mars-scholarship-fund

Heath, Chris. "The Mars Expedition." *GQ*. April 2013. http://www.gq.com/style/wear-it-now/201304/bruno-mars-interview-gq-april-2013

Joaquin, Tannya. "One-on-one with Bruno Mars' dad on his superstar son." *Hawaii News* Now. April 17, 2014. http://www.hawaiinewsnow.com/story/25279858/one-on-one-with-bruno-mars-dad-on-his-superstar-son

Letkemann, Jessica. "Bruno Mars' 10 Biggest Billboard Hits." *Billboard*. January 30, 2014. http://www.billboard.com/articles/list/5892794/bruno-mars-10-biggest-billboard-hits-top-10-songs-charts?utm_source=twitter

Lynn, Bryan. "Bruno Mars' Sisters Talk New Show and Death of Mom." *ET*. November 7, 2013. http://www.etonline.com/tv/140494_Bruno_Mars_Sisters_Talk_The_Lylas_Death_of_Mom/

Newman, Melinda. "Review: Bruno Mars Delivers a Fun, Soulful Halftime Show at Super Bowl XLVIII. "http://www.hitfix.com/news/review-bruno-mars-delivers-a-fun-soulful-halftime-show-at-super-bowl-xlviii

GLOSSARY

brain aneurysm (BREYN AN-yuh-riz-uh-m)–A blood vessel that bursts in the brain.

collaborate (kuh-LAB-uh-reyt)–To work together on a song or project.

demo (DEM-oh)–A recording of a new singer that can be given to recording companies.

episode (EP-i-sood)–One program of a long-running television show.

halftime show–The show between the first and second halves of a football game.

imitate (IM-i-teyt)–to sound like someone or something.

impersonator (im-PUR-se-naa-ter)–A person who can sound like another, usually famous, person.

international (in-ter-NA-shun-al)–Involving several countries.

jukebox (JOOK-boks)–A machine that plays records usually for coins.

medley (MED-lee)–A mixture of songs or parts of songs to make one piece of music.

NFL–National Football League organizes national football games in the US.

opening act–A show that happens before the main show.

outcast (OUT-kast)–A person who feels like they are not included in a group.

paralyzed (PAR-e-liiz-d)–A person who cannot move parts of their body.

reality show–A television show where people are filmed living their everyday lives.

scholarship (SKOL-er-ship)–A money award for the purpose of going to school.

typhoon (TY-foon)–A tropical storm that results in damage to land and buildings.

unorthodox (un-OR-tha-doks)–Someone or something that does not follow the approved way of doing things.

INDEX